THE FEAR
OF HEAVEN

A Play

JOHN MORTIMER

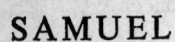

SAMUEL FRENCH

FRENCH

LONDON
NEW YORK TORONTO SYDNEY HOLLYWOOD

THE FEAR OF HEAVEN

First presented at the Greenwich Theatre on the 28th May 1976, with the following cast of characters:

CHARACTERS:

Lewis Luby	Denholm Elliott
Tommy Fletcher	Peter Woodthorpe
Sophie Luby	Hana-Maria Pravda
An English-speaking Guide	Alan Dudley
A Nun	Rita Giovannini
A Doctor	Trevor Baxter
A Young Italian Patient	Leonardo Pieroni

The Play directed by John Tydeman

Setting by Peter Rice

The action takes place in a ward of the Hospital for Transients and the Urban Poor, housed in the ancient Palazzo Martedi in a town in Tuscany

Time—the present

THE FEAR OF HEAVEN

A ward of the Hospital for Transients and the Urban Poor, housed in the ancient Palazzo Martedi in a town in Tuscany

On the ceiling of the ward there is an important painting, "The Fear of Heaven", by Bernadino di Taddeo, named Il Zoppo, painted in the year 1453. At first the stage is in darkness, then a section of the ceiling is lit brilliantly, but we see only a corner of the great picture of Heaven—an impression of a blue sky, floating clouds, green grass and a huge foot in a sandal with the big toe especially prominent—the big toe of God

The Guide comes up from the audience, waving a walking-stick.

He is a seedy man with a slight limp, in a black alpaca jacket stained with spaghetti and cigarette ash. He wears shapeless grey trousers

Guide This way, my group! English spoken! English spoken here! Eyes up, everyone! Upwards. That's what we've come to see. Heaven! "The Fear of Heaven".

It is now possible to see dimly the hospital beds upstage. In the centre two beds are hidden by green screens, from one of which comes the sound of oxygen breathing. In an unscreened bed L, a young Italian is moaning and cursing quietly. A nursing Nun in a white habit enters and goes behind the screen

The fear. That is to say, the awe. You might translate it the "Wonder of Heaven". (*He moves to another position*) We are now directly beneath the feet of God the Father. This is the largest painting of a foot in Italy. God's big toe alone measures over three foot in length. Jolly impressive, isn't it?

The Nun comes out from behind the screen. The Young Italian shouts at her

Italian Patient *Santa Maria! Un orinale.*

The Nun goes off, clucking disapproval

The Guide is pointing at another part of the ceiling

Guide Just look up there on the lawn. Saints and philosophers, no doubt, having some jolly interesting conversations. Please notice the smiles on all those who have passed through the blessed gates.

The Nun returns with a glass bottle

With relief the Young Italian puts it under the bedclothes

In Il Zoppo's beautiful painting of Heaven there are fifty-three varieties of wild flowers, all to be found in the hills of his native Tuscany. There are no fewer than thirty-one varieties of ornamental and singing birds. Quite a zoo, actually. (*He moves and points to another area of the ceiling*)

The Nun leaves with the bottle

In this corner the angels are playing sacred music on their instruments. Notice that they have the faces of good mature women and mothers of families. They are not irresponsible teenagers like the angels of Sandro Botticelli.

The Nun returns with a clipboard; and with Doctor Benjamini, a young Italian of great culture and charm, with horn-rimmed glasses, a white coat and a manner of bored indifference to the patients

The Guide points upwards at a corner of the stage

Over the door please notice the portrait of the Duke Alfonso de Martedi, who built this palace in the year thirteen hundred and ninety-two.

The Nun and Doctor have pushed the screens aside, making a square in the centre of the stage, in which the two central beds stand and we can see their unconscious occupants, their heads propped up by pillows. From where they lie they can only see upwards to the ceiling, the rest of the ward is screened off from their view. They are both English. One is Tommy Fletcher, short, broad, middle-aged, with a small moustache. He is lying breathing irregularly. The oxygen cylinder is standing, unused at the moment, beside his bed. In the next bed, also unconscious, is Lewis Luby, also middle-aged, a lecturer for the British Council. Both men are wearing striped flannel pyjamas. The Doctor feels Fletcher's pulse in an uninterested way

The whole building is now in use by the Government of Italy as a hospital for Transients and the Urban Poor

The Doctor lets Fletcher's wrist drop and moves downstage. The Nun goes and sits down on her chair

You may now admire the ceiling for a few moments of leisure. Please be careful of the hospital equipment.

The Guide goes to the Doctor and offers him a cigarette from a battered packet

Coffin peg, Doctor?
Doctor Grazie, Tanto. How are your tourists, keen?

The Doctor lights their cigarettes with a gold lighter. The Guide coughs into the smoke

Guide They will take their eyes off the ceiling and start peering at the patients.
Doctor True, the patients are a great distraction. I often feel, with you, they spoil the beauty of this remarkable hospital. Today they brought us a couple more, English. You were not at the meeting of the English-Speaking Union at the Palazzo Publico?
Guide (*still coughing*) Bit of jealousy there. I don't get asked.
Doctor Just as well; the balcony collapsed.
Guide I heard a sort of distant boom as we were doing the Martedi tombs. (*Coughing*) Well, I suppose we all end up here eventually.
Doctor In this country we spend far too much trying to patch up our old people and too little, in my opinion, on preserving great works of art. Your visiting lecturer Signor Luby can take comfort. He fell from a balcony attributed to the great Palladio. It's a pleasure to have a man of culture here. Too often they lie with their eyes closed, listening to their radios. (*With disgust*)

They only interest themselves in bed-pans and bottles of
medicine. They never raise their eyes to the Great Work of
Art above them.

Guide Never?

Doctor When they are dead, of course. Only when they are dead.
We notice that the eyes are always directed upwards.

The Doctor stubs out his cigarette and goes

*The Guide squeezes his cigarette out and puts the stub in his breast
pocket for later use. He returns to address his tourists*

Guide All right, my group. Off to the Cathedral. Treats in store
are Giotto's portrait of Santa Catherina and a small quantity
of her liquefied blood. This way, please. Come along, all my
English-speaking group.

The Guide goes

Silence. The Nun starts to knit. The light changes as time passes

Young Italian (*calling from his bed*) Un orinale—per amor di Dio!

Nun (*sharply*) Silencio! Tutti dormano.

*The Young Italian switches on a transistor radio at the side of his
bed. A short burst of Puccini's "Madame Butterfly"*

(*more sharply*) Silencio! Il radio! L'Inglese e molto ammalato!

*The Young Italian clicks off the radio. Silence. Then the sound of a
clock chiming the quarters—it is about to strike the hour. Light
increases on the ceiling which (by an increase of light on it or by a
mechanical movement) seems to become larger and more dominant
over the centre of the stage. At the same time the centre square
between the screens becomes lighter and the rest of the ward more
shadowy. Mr Luby starts to stir and speaks*

Luby For the poet, madame—incest isn't a crime. It's a necessity!

The clock strikes—one

What? What's that . . .? That bell? Where am I? *Where?* (*He
feels for his glasses at the side of the bed, puts them on and
looks up at the ceiling—then he sits up, panic stricken*) No! Not
here! It's impossible. Quite impossible. (*Appalled*) Oh, my God!
You exist . . .! (*Pause; he suddenly shouts*) This is Luby here!

Lewis Luby! Atheist and man of letters! I have rejected you—
completely! I mean, even—even if ... You have defied the
laws of probability. And of science ... You won't want me
here, I'm sure. There's been a mistake ... A serious mistake.
(*Louder*) A mistake! Can you hear me? (*Deeply worried*)
Angels. Actually angels. Playing harps! This is quite absurd.
It's high time I said—something outrageous. Wipe that serene
look off their faces. (*He gets out of bed and calls up at the ceiling*)
You! You over there! *Madame. Signora. Senora. Liebe.
Frau!* My name is Luby and I am quite unable to find the
slightest evidence of life after death. Did you hear that, all of
you? I have never for one moment believed in the immor-
tality of the soul! Let alone, let alone—this place! Well, you
don't think the mere fact of being dead's going to change my
mind, do you? I tell you, Lewis Luby's not so easily persuaded!
You know my opinions, don't you? You've followed them, no
doubt—with those all-seeing eyes of yours. I am the author of
*The Prince of Darkness, A Study of Lord Byron as a Sexual
Outcast, Baudelaire and the Satanists, Swinburne and the
Divine Marquis de Sade.* Did your omniscience happen to
notice my piece on "Poetry of the Damned" last week in the
Times Lit. Supp.? Did that raise a few celestial eyebrows, did
it? (*Pause*) You're very quiet. You think—I'm being frivolous,
don't you? Luby flippant again. Luby doesn't take things
seriously. Well, I *don't!* I have no intention of taking this
seriously. This is an optical illusion. There's some quite
simple scientific explanation. I tell you what it is. Exactly!
It's a bad dream, brought on by over-indulgence in British
Council sherry and too much of that dubious fish paste spread
on cheesy biscuits. I am going to shut my eyes now and count
to ten. (*He sits down on the bed and shuts his eyes*) By the time I
open them again you will have all gone away! Vanished!
You ... You old Myth, you ... Fairy tales! *Opiate of the
People!* One—two—three ...

Fletcher (*sleepily; speaking with a Humberside accent, without
opening his eyes*) Who's that? Who?

Luby Four—five—six ...

Fletcher Gwen? Is that my little Gwenny ...?

Luby Seven—eight ...

Fletcher Alison ...? Jimbo. Is that you, Jim boy?

Luby Nine . . . I said nine . . .

Fletcher Just slipped into the chemist—on the hunt for Fly Death . . .

Luby All right. Are you ready? Ten!

Fletcher Bloody Iti chemist. Pulled a knife on yours truly. I must've upset them somehow . . .

Luby *Ten!* I said ten!

Fletcher Did you say ten?

Luby Vanish! Pack up your ridiculous harps and vanish!

Fletcher (*opening his eyes and looking out at Luby*) Look, friend. I'm not interfering with you, am I? Just had a spot of bother with one of the natives round in the chemists.

Luby also opens his eyes, and looks up at the ceiling

Luby I don't believe it for a moment. You're still there! (*He stands to examine the ceiling more closely*)

Fletcher Yes. And here I'll stay. Got me in the gut, most probably. All the same—I thought it'd've been more painful. I didn't feel much really. No pain to speak of . . .

Luby Harps! I just can't bear the thought of the Archbishop of Canterbury arriving here. That awful smug "I told you so" expression.

Fletcher Can you help me, friend?

Luby looks at Fletcher then moves to him

Luby It's a fellow soul. Calling me "friend" . . .

Fletcher Can you just help me get my bearings?

Luby "Friend"? Is that what they call each other here? Like a Baptist congress in Philadelphia. (*Very depressed, he sits down on his bed*)

Fletcher Pardon me, old man. Where are we?

Luby Oh, where do you think?

Fletcher Search me . . .

Luby Look. Up there—look upwards. (*Pause*) Well?

Fletcher looks up at the ceiling. Pause. He is amazed

Fletcher Oh. My God!

Luby Yours perhaps. He's never been mine.

Fletcher (*in an awestruck whisper*) Tell me frankly. Have we passed over?

Luby That would seem an appropriate cliché for an extremely trite situation.

Pause. Fletcher climbs out of bed; he looks up at the ceiling

Fletcher (*awestruck*) It's beautiful!

Luby You think so?

Fletcher Beautifully kept. Like the Municipal Gardens without the begonias.

Luby That seems a suitably depressing description.

Fletcher Quite a fair area of grass, isn't there?

Luby If you like grass there is quite a lot of it. Yes.

Fletcher Take a bit of mowing, that area of lawn.

Luby I don't imagine there's much else to do here. I see it as a perpetual English Sunday . . .

Fletcher Those angels. They look pleasant enough.

Luby (*contemptuously*) Pleasant! I have always preferred the corrupt innocence of those misnamed Ladies of Pleasure— Dark Angels. I have often missed stations—following one on the Northern Line . . .

Fletcher I imagine time will pass—very pleasantly up here.

Luby Oh, yes! Picture the evenings? Gounod's *Ave Maria* on the West lawn and readings from *The Little Flowers of St Francis*.

Fletcher (*suddenly shouting*) Hallelujah!

Luby (*revolted*) Oh, please!

Fletcher (*whispering*) Isn't that what you're meant to say?

Luby I have no idea. I arrived here rather suddenly.

Fletcher (*sitting down on his bed*) You only recently—passed over?

Luby One moment I was taking sherry and cheesy biscuits with a perfectly civilized old trout from the American Library. We were discussing, as I remember it, the various sexual contre-temps of the great Lord Byron and the theme of damnation in Romantic Poetry. Suddenly there was a cry of warning from a startled cleric who had disapproved of my lecture. "Look out, chaps. The balcony's falling in!" I only had time for a last gulp of the South African Amontillado before they dumped me in this celestial kindergarten.

Fletcher You felt—no pain at all?

Luby Very little.

Fletcher It doesn't seem to hurt much. Not death.

Luby Oh, I agree. It's the life after that's such agony.

Fletcher You shouldn't say that!

Luby Why?

Fletcher It's ungrateful!

Luby I never asked to come here!

Fletcher Of course you didn't. It's an honour. Like sitting at the Master Mason's table at the annual dinner dance.

Luby That seems to sum it up pretty accurately.

Fletcher Be thankful. Look around you! It's just like the pictures in Sunday School.

Luby I know nothing about that, of course.

Fletcher Don't you remember them?

Luby My dear mother was Chairlady of the Dulwich Humanitarians. I'd've gone to Sunday School over her dead body.

Fletcher And now you've come here over yours! Pardon my sense of humour.

Luby No doubt your little jokes will make eternity pass extremely slowly.

Fletcher Eternity? I imagine we'll be here for quite some time.

Luby Not me. Not once they realize the mistake they're making.

Fletcher Well. We might as well get to know each other. The name's Fletcher. The boys call me Tommy. What's yours?

Pause

Luby What? Oh, I'm Luby. Lewis Luby. Does it ring a bell?

Fletcher I'm afraid—not a tinkle.

Luby *The* Lewis Luby. Of *The Prince of Darkness, Lord Byron as a Sexual Outcast.*

Fletcher Unusual name.

Luby I'm an unusual person.

Fletcher I'm not. Very ordinary. Can't imagine why I should get sent here.

Luby Perhaps as a reward for an uneventful life.

Fletcher I haven't been *that* charitable. Odd flag on Life Boat Day, of course. Charity begins at home—and you need it after what the tax man leaves you. I had a diabolical coding!

Luby Mr Fletcher. I don't intent to spend the next ten thousand years discussing your income tax!

Fletcher Oh, I beat the P.A.Y.E. all right. Once I emigrated to

the land of spaghetti and kissed the Inland Revenue good-bye.
It seems they don't hold that against you. Not up here.

Luby Perhaps they don't know. The place doesn't look exactly
staffed with Chartered Accountants.

Fletcher They know everything. And they forgive you. That's
what it is. 'Course I've done a bit for export. That might count
in my favour.

Luby (*uninterestedly*) Really?

Fletcher Meat pies and pin tables. I run the English café down by
the old Marina. We do an all-in meal and a bingo evening plus
amusements for ten thousand lire. We made a good thing of it.

Luby You think that earned you Salvation—like the Queen's
reward for industry?

Fletcher What else worked it? I'm no saint.

Luby And I, Fletcher, am certainly a sinner.

Fletcher Ssh . . .

Luby I have no intention of keeping quiet about it.

Fletcher No point in reminding Him, if it's all water under the
bridge. No point in raising old embarrassments. That *is* God
the Father, isn't it, Mr Luby? I mean from where we are now
you don't see much past the sandal.

Luby I imagine He will be looking presently, in this direction.

Fletcher I thought I recognized Him, from the pictures . . .

Luby (*standing up and shouting at God's foot*)
    "*Mais le Damné répond*
    Toujours 'Je ne veux pas!' "

Fletcher (*puzzled*) What?

Luby "The damned still answer
    We want no part of Heaven!"
    You have no French?

Fletcher None whatsoever.

Luby What is this place? A public park stocked with people who
don't know their Baudelaire.

Fletcher Am I?

Luby What?

Fletcher Whatever you said.

Luby Oh, my God!

Fletcher (*reverenlty*) Well, at least you can pray. That's something.

Luby You'll be telling me next you are entirely ignorant of Lord B.

Fletcher Who?

Luby George Gordon Noel. The Lord Byron.

Fletcher *The Lord Byron* I know well.

Luby Oh, really? Are you one of his intimates, Fletcher? One of his devil-may-care cronies? Did you share the housemaids with his Lordship at Newstead Abbey, or the boys in Venice, or did you just drink and gamble the night away in his rooms in St James?

Fletcher It's a motel . . .

Luby What?

Fletcher *The Lord Byron.* The new motel, outside Nottingham, on the A Forty-six.

Luby (*desperately*) There is no culture here!

Fletcher A cosy sort of place. Me and my little Gwenny stayed there, on occasion. Double bed with shower and no luggage asked for.

Luby Lord Byron, Fletcher, has absolutely nothing to do with you and your little Gwenny. Lord Byron was a great poet who shouted his defiance at the heavens—and sinned gloriously. And I have lit candles at the altar of his wickedness in a hundred lectures specially given for the British Council—both sides of the Iron Curtain.

Fletcher (*suspiciously*) You give lectures?

Luby I prefer to think of them, as small acts of liberation.

Fletcher With slides, would that be?

During the following speech Fletcher looks more and more shocked

Luby (*pacing and gesturing eloquently*) I do not need slides! I rely on words and the poet's great example. "Experience", I tell my listeners, "is the only duty of the artist. All experience is an arch where-through—glimmers the unknown truth. It is the duty of the artist to live life to the full!" I tell them quite honestly. His destiny and his curse! The poet must be mad, bad and dangerous to know. He finds his inspiration waking between two greasy whores in Seven Dials or watching the sun set over Mont Blanc—among the monks of Athos and the boys catamites of Syracuse, dancing in a Venetian carnival or vomiting in the gutters of Piccadilly.

Fletcher (*appalled*) You actually used that word?

Luby What word?

Fletcher "Vomiting".

Luby The divine nausea that follows each inspired Bacchanalia.

Fletcher Filthy!

Luby "We gaze into a puddle—and see the reflections of the stars."

Fletcher Mixed lectures, I imagine they are.

Luby As mixed as possible.

Fletcher You *devil!*

Luby (*pleased*) Thank you, Fletcher, I do my best. The devil has all the best lines in Milton . . .

Fletcher It's immoral!

Luby Art has no moral boundaries! That's what I tell them.

Fletcher Flaunting it. In public. Who pays for it? That's what I'd like to know.

Luby What?

Fletcher Who finances you—spreading that muck around the world? I know—Jo Muggins!

Luby Who?

Fletcher Me! The British Tax Payer!

Luby I thought you had resigned from that position . . .

Fletcher I'm still entitled to my voice, aren't I? As one of the silent majority.

Luby I think there may be some logical flaw in that statement.

Fletcher To see that certain standards are maintained! Suppose— suppose a child happened to walk into one of your lectures.

Luby Children seldom stray into talks on Romantic Poetry in a foreign language.

Fletcher A young girl might go in thinking it was Brownies . . .

Luby Your ingenuity amazes me.

Fletcher Our kids are entitled to a little childhood, Mr Luby.

Luby I knew it! I knew heaven'd be like this! Let's hope Mrs Whitehouse isn't feeling seedy.

Luby lies on the bed as if suddenly bored with the argument

Fletcher Whatever I've done. I haven't gone around trumpeting it from the podium. I haven't flashed it on the screen in the form of lantern slides.

Luby I told you. There are *no* lantern slides!

Fletcher I'm not setting up as perfect but at least I've caused no offence . . .

Luby I imagine your life has been as free from offence as the expurgated edition of *Little Women*.

Fletcher I mean, I may have taken Gwenny down to the motel a week-end or two. But we did our best not to cause embarrassment. I always treated Gwen like a sister . . .

Luby Hardly a romantic approach to your mistress.

Fletcher I don't see why. After all she *was* my sister.

Pause. Luby sits up slowly and looks at Fletcher

Luby She was—*what?*

Fletcher My sister.

Luby Mr Fletcher. Why are you telling me this?

Fletcher I don't want you to get the idea I'm not completely normal.

Luby (*puzzled*) Normal?

Fletcher (*determinedly, standing up*) I mean, a man with just the usual desires and instincts. I can't stand filth, that's all. There's not a lecture you can take the family to these days. It's shocking!

Luby It was your sister you took away . . . ?

Fletcher (*looking up at the ceiling*) It's been forgiven, surely? Seeing I'm here.

Luby Your sister Gwen?

Fletcher Ten years younger than me—and slim as a daffodil. The flesh is weak, Mr Luby.

Luby I imagine so. Given the opportunity.

Fletcher Our Gwen was always a nervous child in company. She'd sit at a family tea as good as gold, never get a word out of her except "thank you" for a piece of cake. But when it was over she'd be out with me for a walk along the sands dancing like a wild thing and laughing at the Aunts.

Luby (*confused*) You lived by the sea?

Fletcher Humberside. You know it at all?

Luby Hardly at all.

Fletcher Fine sands. Little dunes with tufts of grass on them. Naturally one thing led to another.

Luby I've found—one thing has so often led to nothing.

Fletcher I could make Gwen laugh so easily. You know how it is. That's all you want, isn't it, a bit of a laugh and then you're away. Any woman's the same.

Luby My own wife doesn't laugh very much. She comes from Austria. (*Pause*) But, Mr Fletcher. Are you quite sure—you read no poetry?

Fletcher None whatsoever. I hardly get time for the newspaper.

Luby Then how do you explain it?

Fletcher Explain what, Mr Luby?

Luby That in certain respects you and the great Lord B . . . Well, in *one* respect at least . . . (*Hopefully*) I assume this remarkable close family relationship has been your only peccadillo?

Fletcher (*sitting down on his bed, facing Luby*) I was never *really* unfaithful to Gwenny . . .

Luby Ah . . .

Fletcher Not in my heart, I wasn't.

Luby Your heart?

Fletcher I mean, after I married Alison . . .

Luby Alison?

Fletcher The present Mrs Fletcher. She's a qualified book-keeper is Alison. Helped me build up the business . . .

Luby A mathematician?

Fletcher Computer sharp.

Luby Hard, cold, angular? The Princess of the Parallelograms?

Fletcher Soft, dark and kindness itself.

Luby But in her heart somewhere—a chip of ice? Not a passionate woman, your mathematical wife?

Fletcher Nothing wrong with my Alison, in the bed department.

Luby Nothing?

Fletcher Warm, crisp and regular. Like a slice of breakfast toast.

Luby But your little Gwen . . .

Fletcher It was the laughs I had with Gwenny. She saw the joke in everything. Whatever I said I got the laughs out of her, like hitting the jackpot.

Luby So you still went walking across the sands?

Fletcher Most Fridays. When Alison had an evening casting up the books.

Luby Tell me, Mr Fletcher. Tell me quite honestly. Weren't you afraid of *La Grande Scandale*?

Fletcher People talking?

Luby Exactly!

Fletcher I took precautions . . .

Luby You were discreet?

Fletcher It was the year I heard a certain whispering at a Chamber of Commerce function. I had to put an end to the rumours. I arranged for Gwen to marry Jimbo.

Luby (*frowning*) I don't think we've heard of Jimbo, have we?

Fletcher Jim Penrose. We were at school together.

Luby A life long friend?

Fletcher He was a lad, was Jimbo. Good at everything!

Luby First prize for Algebra *and* on the cricket field?

Fletcher Hit like a County player. Cut into the water like a swallow, top of the wall bars as soon as look at you—and if it was any kind of mischief . . .

Luby Stink bombs, itching powder? Plastic doggy-do on the altar steps . . . ?

Fletcher Lovers! Jim had all the lovers . . .

Luby You went to a co-educational school, then? Just like mine . . .

Fletcher One sex strictly. You never got a sight of a girl at the Grammar.

Luby So your Jim's lovers . . .

Fletcher Queued up! I was lucky to be one of them. I was a duffer at cricket . . .

Luby And Jim confined himself, mainly to the first eleven?

Fletcher I was the exception. I don't know why. My sense of humour must have tickled him . . .

Luby (*disapprovingly, standing up*) Your sense of humour seems to have brought you many opportunities . . .

Fletcher Oh yes—I think it's because of that Jim stuck to me, even after school . . .

Luby You continued to meet?

Fletcher At Masonic functions, old school reunions. Jim went into the motor trade. I was in catering. There was bags of opportunities . . .

Luby I'm sorry. I begin to be appalled.

Fletcher We took up angling. Jim made some fantastic catches, naturally I was a duffer. If anyone saw us walking up the sand together of an evening we were out after bait. You know, those small worms that make wedding cake decorations on the sand . . .

Luby I *don't* know.

Fletcher You put down a drop of salt and fool the worms into thinking the tide's come in . . .

Luby Cunning, no doubt! So you had the best of three worlds?

Fletcher It was like a fast ride on a motor bike with Gwen. And my Alison was always a comfort. But when it came to Jimbo . . .

Luby Well?

Fletcher Jim was—like keeping young forever.

Luby (*turning on Fletcher, horrified*) So it was Jim you persuaded to marry Gwen?

Fletcher When people started talking. It didn't make any difference, of course, not to any of us!

Luby Life continued—much as before?

Fletcher Business as usual. Until the tax man got at us. Then I moved them all out here.

Luby Everyone?

Fletcher The whole family! We work as a team.

Luby Obviously.

Fletcher Down by the old Marina! *La Trattoria Tommy.* Gwenny's behind the bar and Jim's clickety click.

Luby So I understood you to say.

Fletcher He calls the numbers on Thursdays. And Alison does the books, naturally. They'll be wondering where I've got to . . .

Luby (*sarcastically*) I really can't imagine what they'll do without you.

Fletcher No. They'd all be glad, though. To know I arrived here safely . . .

Luby I should think they'll be astonished!

Fletcher Astonished? Why? I've done nothing to be ashamed of.

Luby Nothing to be . . . ? Mr Fletcher, I told you. I'm not easily shocked! In fact I should have said up till now I was unshockable. But I find your conduct inexcusable!

Fletcher *They* didn't. Not up here.

Luby What they think or do up here really doesn't affect me in the slightest. What you have revealed is a life of pure self-indulgence!

Fletcher (*standing up and facing him*) What about that Lord B of yours you're always on about? Boys in Venice—greasy whores . . .

Luby The poet Byron lived for his art!

Fletcher Didn't stop his fun, though, did it?

Luby Fun? What do you mean, fun? It was his martyrdom. So far as I can see you have indulged your appalling sensuality simply because you enjoy it . . .

Fletcher Seems a good reason . . .

Luby And you have not produced from your sordid intrigues one sonnet! Not a quatrain. Not even taken time in your prancing from bed to bed, regardless of age and sex, to jot down a single rhyming couplet. How can you justify it?

Fletcher I kept them happy.

Luby Happiness—is not everything. Are artists happy?

Fletcher I was.

Luby Your conduct strikes me, as entirely selfish.

Fletcher I was thinking of *them*.

Luby Oh, really?

Fletcher I'm not saying I've always kept on the straight and narrow. A man has to have *something* outside his family life.

Luby Even with your extended family?

Fletcher But when I thought that business with young Claudia got out of hand . . .

Luby *Claudia?* (*He turns away from him, disgusted*) Your life swells to epic proportions, Fletcher. With a cast of thousands!

Fletcher Her husband runs the chemists down the Corso Garibaldi. We get all sorts of insects down the coast in the summer. I often call in for a bomb of Fly Death when I'm in town. Good stuff, that Fly Death. I can recommend it . . .

Luby Mr Fletcher! (*Turning back to him*) Now you're here— now by some extraordinary lattitude on the part of the authorities you've scraped your way into Heaven—I imagine you'll have as little use for Fly Death as for your undoubted talent for intrigue and romance . . . !

Fletcher It was all right at first. We had a lot of fun. She'd lock the shop up and we'd go in there, behind the bead curtain. But then she started coming down the Trat on Sundays, making scenes. One day she upset the Bingo. I couldn't have Alison worried.

Luby Or Gwen? Or Jimbo, presumably?

Fletcher I called to tell her it was all over. She ran to get the knife out of the kitchen and came back screaming. Luckily I can't speak much of the lingo.

Luby You might have been shocked?

Fletcher It was uncalled for, what she did. Definitely uncalled for. I hardly felt it. That's what surprised me.

Fletcher sits down on his bed again as if feeling weak

Luby "How foreign women revenge". If you'd bothered to read Lord Byron . . .

Fletcher They don't watch what they're doing. Seen them drive, haven't you? She wasn't in full control of the knife.

Luby There seems to me to be a certain natural justice . . .

Fletcher Justice?

Luby You were heading for trouble, if you want my opinion. You'd simply got away with it too long.

Fletcher But I thought you took the view . . .

Luby A poet's life without a line of poetry to show for it! Oh yes, Mr Fletcher, I'm afraid you rather had it coming.

Fletcher I'm no worse than the rest of you.

Luby (*with growing indignation*) We don't all flee the country, Mr Fletcher, to avoid the tax man and set up unisex harems in foreign bingo halls. Incest and homosexuality are not our regular diversions, like the *Times* crossword. We don't drop into the chemists in the afternoon for a small packet of aspirins and a spot of adultery.

Fletcher You must have done it often.

Luby (*outraged*) I *must!* Must I? Let me tell you, Fletcher. With the single exception of Mrs Luby I've never had a woman in my life! (*He sits down on his bed*)

Pause. Then Fletcher bursts into loud, uncontrollable laughter

Have I said something particularly amusing?

Fletcher (*trying to control himself*) You—old sinner, you! "The devil has all the best lines". Isn't that what you told me . . . ?

Luby I was discussing the poetry of Milton . . .

Fletcher (*incredulously*) You mean *no-one*—only your good lady?

Luby No-one else at all. (*Pause*) Naturally, I'm sensitive about it. (*Pause*) It's not the sort of thing, one likes to have generally known.

Fletcher They'd think you were kinky down our Rotary! (*Starting to laugh again*) I'm sorry.

Luby I shouldn't have told you. You led me into it.

Fletcher But it's unbelievable!

Luby Yes, it is rather. I suppose it is.

Fletcher I'm beginning to think—you haven't ever lived, Mr Luby!

Luby I was meaning to. I was looking forward to it . . .

Fletcher But you must have had bags of opportunity, from your early years.

Luby Not really, a great deal of opportunity.

Fletcher I mean, I was brought up strictly Chapel. My Dad never missed the Radio Parson. But *you*, Mr Luby. With a mother who let you off Sunday School. An unbeliever!

Luby Mother! Poor Mother. She put no moral pressure on me. She gave me no rules. She only said that if I did anything "ugly", it would make her very sad.

Fletcher And did you?

Luby Oh, believe me, Mr Fletcher. I spent my early years desperately hunting for an opportunity to make Mother sad.

Fletcher So as soon as you got to your school . . .

Luby She sent me to a co-educational day place. Run by Quakers.

Fletcher You mean, girls in the classes?

Luby I was a nervous boy, desperately shy and frightened of cricket balls. The girls were only interested in sport . . .

Fletcher Like my Jimbo.

Luby They bowled me out first ball in the nets and from then on ignored me.

Fletcher So—you never took advantage?

Luby Nothing happened. Mother remained imperturbably happy.

Fletcher But sometime, surely . . .

Luby I hesitated. It seemed for an eternity.

Fletcher Don't want to waste your time. Life's too short.

Luby Oh, I agree. At last I decided that I was the Captain of my Soul. I'd take my life and throw it on the table. To win or lose all! I would enlist in the Army of the Condemned! I remember it as if it were yesterday. I put on a clean white shirt, open at the neck with a paisley scarf—part of Mother's personal effects. I splashed on eau-de-cologne—it was before the age of after-shave, you follow me?

Fletcher Pleased to. I've made similar preparations.

Luby It was a poetry evening at the Literary Institute. Mulled wine was being served, and Dundee cake.

Fletcher Some kind of an orgy? You'll get that with poets . . .

Luby I looked round. It was the period of dirndl skirts and embroidered blouses. The lady poets looked big and healthy, glowing, I thought, like Byron's peasant maids . . . "With breasts never made to suckle slaves . . ." Mother was forgotten! I owed experience a debt which could only be paid with my virginity.

Fletcher And you were, how old, exactly?

Luby Exactly? It was my thirty-first birthday. I looked about the room and prepared to make a decision. The decision that would alter my whole life! The green dirndl in the corner, I thought— or the soft brown eyes, the red sweater and strong white teeth about to sink into a doorstep of cake . . . I paused to make my selection. And then . . .

Fletcher Then?

Luby A hand fell on my arm like an arrest. I was offered a glass of mulled wine in an Austrian accent. I had been selected.

Fletcher By?

Luby Sophie. The present Mrs Luby. She simply wouldn't take "no" for an answer.

Fletcher And you?

Luby Married her. It was what she preferred.

Fletcher Well, I'm sure you found some sort of occasion. Some sort of evening off. The Masons perhaps, or the Rotary. Then slip away early . . .

Luby I never once deceived her.

Fletcher Never on any occasion?

Luby Never.

Fletcher Let's get this clear . . .

Luby Yes . . .

Fletcher You were totally inexperienced at the age of thirty-one?

Luby Totally.

Fletcher And then—it was only your wife . . . ?

Luby No-one but Sophie. You've forced the disgraceful truth out of me.

Fletcher stands up and looks up at the ceiling thoughtfully

Fletcher No wonder they put you in here, Mr Luby.

Luby (*standing up, outraged*) Don't say it! I am here because of my appalling record. I am one of the sexually underprivileged.

It was my upbringing—the accident of myopia and a slight
stoop. Even so I could have risen above my disadvantages. I
could never have been Byron, of course—but a more modest
form of dissolute poet—Ernest Dawson, perhaps. I could have
managed. "I have been faithful to thee, Cynara, in my fashion
. . ." Sophie wouldn't put up with infidelity.

Fletcher How did she stop you?

Luby (*sitting down; disconsolately*) She said that it would make
her sad.

Fletcher Like your . . .

Luby Her sadness was terrible! Days of thunder and the rivulets
of tears. Our living-room became a sort of wailing wall on the
one occasion I was late home.

Fletcher You'd been following those Ladies of Pleasure . . .

Luby For a station or two on the tube only. I came to my senses
around Mornington Crescent.

Fletcher But still she carried on.

Luby I never kept her waiting after that . . .

Fletcher But when you came away. Like on lectures?

Fletcher sits down beside Luby on Luby's bed

Luby She expected a postcard daily. I never had the courage
to deceive her on a postcard. You see what my life's been, Mr
Fletcher?

Fletcher I suppose you could say, on the quietish side.

Luby To be landed here. In this uneventful eternity!

Fletcher Like finding the bar closed before you ever got round to
ordering a drink.

Luby Mr Fletcher . . .

Fletcher Yes?

Luby You know, that really puts it rather well.

Fletcher Thank you.

Pause

Luby I was no doubt a little hard on you.

Fletcher Think nothing of it.

Luby A little—over-critical.

Fletcher That surprised me, rather.

Luby You must understand—I'm a little edgy. A little piqued. I
have suffered—a considerable disappointment.

Fletcher Disappointment, Mr Luby?

Luby Finding myself—so unexpectedly in heaven . . .

Fletcher Indeed, yes. I do see. I see it must be, something of a let-down for you.

Luby To be unexpectedly taken off—in a state of innocence! To pass from one uneventful eternity to another . . . To be called to rest, Mr Fletcher, before one has a chance of getting tired.

Pause

Fletcher (*yawning and stretching*) I think I was about ready for it. (*He moves over to his bed*)

Luby What?

Fletcher (*getting back into his bed, pulling up the covers over him, preparing for sleep*) The whistle. I've enjoyed the game, of course. Every minute of it. Alison and Claudia and Jimbo and Gwendoline. Especially young Gwen. But they seem to want more out of you as the years go by. It even got just that much more of an effort to make young Gwen laugh. Yes. I'm not sorry to be packing it all in.

Luby "We'll go no more a roving . . ."

Fletcher I'd like a chance of sleeping alone. After all these years.

Luby You should get plenty of that up here.

Fletcher To stretch out your legs right across the bed, to suck boiled sweets and read the Sunday papers. Not to have to climb the stairs each night to a kind of athletic meeting at Wembley Stadium.

Luby Were they so demanding?

Fletcher Time consuming, I'd say. I got no gardening done.

Luby "Though the night was made for loving
    And the moon shines bright . . ."

Fletcher I'd like to have got in more gardening.

Luby Perhaps they'll let you help out with the lawns.

Fletcher I'd appreciate that.

Luby "Though the sword outwears its sheath
    And the soul wears out the breast."

Fletcher (*suspiciously*) What's that mean?

Luby What?

Fletcher "The sword outwears the sheath." What's that intended for?

Luby I imagine its symbolic. Of the poet's virility . . .

Fletcher (*with deep disapproval*) I thought so!

Luby "And the heart must pause to breathe
    And love itself have rest."

Fletcher Disgusting! That's what it is. "The sword wears out the
    sheath." Ought to be put a stop to! (*He closes his eyes*)

Luby "Though the night was made for loving
    And the day returns too soon."

Fletcher (*his voice sonnding faint*) Filth!

Luby "Yes, we'll go no more a roving." (*Shouting*) Oh God!
    Don't you understand? *I never went!* (*More quietly pleading*)
    Let me out. Please. God. Let me back again.

The sound of Gounod's "Ave Maria" is heard

    No! I won't believe it. I won't . . .

*Luby gets back into bed quickly, pulls the bedclothes over his head
and lies down. The lights, including the light on the ceiling, fades
almost to darkness*

    *As the light fades so the Nun moves in and we see her move the
    screen round Fletcher's bed so that he is hidden from the audience.
    Darkness. "Ave Maria" grows louder. The Light changes to
    pale daylight. The ceiling is shadowy and unlit. We can see
    the surrounding ward. The Young Italian's transistor is on,
    playing "Ave Maria". The Nun is standing by the doorway. She
    claps her hands severely*

Nun *Silencio! Il radio. Il dottore arriva!*

The young Italian clicks off his radio

    The Doctor comes in briskly. The Nun goes

The Doctor moves to Luby's bed and touches his shoulder

Doctor Good morning, Mr Luby. Feeling a little better?

Luby (*peering miserably out of the bed covers*) I'll never feel
    better here. Never . . .

Doctor All the same, you seem to be still with us. Lying on your
    back, that's good. Admiring the ceiling?

Luby (*puzzled*) The ceiling?

Doctor I like it best in the early morning. Before the guides come—and the tours. When you are alone watching it one almost feels, does one not, transported to Paradise.

Luby *Almost?*

Doctor Such is the power of a great work of art.

Luby Work of art. Is that all it is?

Doctor *All?* Did you say all? And you a distinguished lecturer. For the British Council. What should we prize more highly— than a superb mural, a masterpiece of the *cinquecento*, the *chef d'oeuvre* of a son of this very city, Bernadino di Taddeo. Nicknamed the lame one. . .

Luby It's *not* heaven?

Doctor Nicknamed "Il Zoppo".

Luby (*sitting up*) Where am I then? *Where?* If it's not heaven it must be . . . Tell me—tell me, my dear fellow. Do you happen to know a Lord Byron? He must be here somewhere. A pale gentleman with black curls. You haven't seen him? Possibly tricked out in Greek National Dress . . .

Doctor Please, Mr Luby . . .

Luby Not with a limp exactly. But with, shall we say, a slight impediment of the leg?

Doctor Calm yourself! I shall have to ask the Nursing Sister to give you a suppository.

Luby (*convinced*) Then I *am* in Hell . . .

Doctor Don't talk nonsense. You are nowhere of the sort.

Luby Nowhere . . .

Doctor You are in the Hospital for Transients and the Urban Poor. Where they brought you last night. After the balcony collapsed . . .

Luby What exactly are you trying to tell me?

Doctor Courage, Mr Luby. You're making a good recovery.

Luby Are you dropping the hint—I'm alive?

Doctor As alive, Mr Luby, as ever.

Luby Alive! (*Excitedly*) Oh, no. More than ever . . .! More! I shall be more alive than ever now. Much more! I have wasted my time! Totally wasted. There's a little more time, isn't there? What do they call it in bars? Drinking up time! No, naturally. You wouldn't know that expression. And I tell you, Doctor. I promise you. I shall drink up everything. Every little drop available!

The Nun returns and stands by the Doctor

For—instance. Let me think now. What they might be serving.
No sister. I have no sister. Mother has a lot to answer for!
Never mind! The world is full. I shall ask everyone! What do
ten refusals matter, ten slaps in the face? Many will refuse but
many will accept. Many will be delighted to accept. What is
there here? What's ready to hand? Nuns. Well, perhaps not
nuns. Not nuns to start with. But there are—chemist shops
no doubt. Doctor—no doubt you know the Corso Garibaldi.
I must go down to the chemists.

*Luby starts to try to get out of bed. The Doctor forces him back as
the Nun whispers a message to the Doctor*

Doctor Mister Luby! What are you trying to do?

*The Doctor nods to the Nun, who goes back to the doorway. Luby
is still struggling to get out of bed*

Luby To enjoy a number of experiences, Doctor! Before its
altogether too late. To collect a few memories, to warm my
old age. Am I still to go to bed with nothing but my wife and
Dame Enid Starkie's *Life of Baudelaire*? Let me get up,
Doctor. I can walk. I suppose I can walk . . . Is there somewhere
here to get a bath—a clean shirt and a whiff of eau-de-cologne?
Let me get up!

Doctor Please! Don't disturb yourself, Mister Luby.

*The Nun comes back with Sophie Luby, a formidable-looking
lady wearing a lot of scarves and beads*

Doctor Look—Sister is bringing you a visitor. A lady.

Luby To visit me? A lady? What lady?

Sophie (*in a rather hearty, cheerful but commanding Austrian
accent,* Lie down now, Lewis. There's a good chap!

Luby (*quietly*) Sophie! You shouldn't have come.

Sophie That's better. Lewis, how could you make me so terribly
sad?

Sophie sits down beside the bed

The Doctor smiles at Sophie, and leaves with the Nun

All night in the aeroplane. In the bus also. I was crying. Crying . . . (*Starting to get tearful*) Oh, Lewis. Why should you do such a thing to your Sophie?

Luby Please don't do that! Try not to weep! I didn't hurl myself from the balcony, you know. It wasn't an act of deliberate defenestration. Designed to cause you distress! In fact, I might say, the whole thing came as a total surprise to me.

Sophie (*determinedly*) You must not go on these tours again.

Luby (*surprised*) I mustn't?

Sophie These lectures! For you they are far too dangerous. I have decided with the lady from the British Council. They will keep you at home now. I have had you grounded old chap.

Luby Home? No, Sophie. Please. I can't stay at home. You see, after this—after this life—it seems we can expect . . . nothing very exciting. I've only got a few years. To make the best of it.

Sophie But it will be exciting, Lewis. I have thought it all out. You shall stay at home and write the definitive book on your old chum the great Lord Byron. Your beloved chap! I will help you. I will type out all your references on little cards. I will keep it systematic! We will have everything in alphabetical order—like for instance his debts—his incest—his homosexual tendencies . . . Oh, Lewis. I will be your right hand man!

Luby But Sophie. I would only experience sin in a card index.

Sophie Well, of course. We would work together. I would have you at home at lunch time. I could get us a salad.

Luby (*bitterly*) A salad! And in the evenings what would we look forward to?

Sophie I make a little chicken dish maybe, how you like it. We'll get some new records for the winter—and books. There are still so many books for us to read together, Lewis. I have been thinking. Should we explore together the relationship of Rimbaud and Verlaine? A couple of queer fish, these two. After your own heart, eh?

Luby (*depressed*) We shall sit together, reading books in the evenings.

Sophie Yes, Lewis. You won't go away from me again! Not ever. Won't that be heaven?

Pause, then Luby answers her, desperate

Luby Heaven?

Sophie (*laughing*) Afraid! Don't be afraid, Lewis. We'll have such a perfect time . . .

Luby Perfect! For all eternity. I think—I need a little advice. Mr Fletcher . . .

Sophie Who? Who do you want?

Luby There was a man here with me. In the next bed. Mr Fletcher. (*He looks at the screen round Fletcher's bed*)

Sophie Who?

Luby (*getting out of bed*) An Englishman. An extraordinary man really . . .

Sophie (*standing up, protesting*) Lewis! You're not well . . . You . . .

Ignoring her, Luby crosses to the screen

Luby Gave his name as Fletcher.

Luby pulls the screen aside. The bed is stripped and empty. The blankets neatly folded. He calls out

Sister! *Sorella! Senta!* Nurse!

The Nun enters and goes to him

Nun *Eccomi, signore.*

Luby *Sorella! Dove L'Inghlese . . . Dove il signore . . .* Tommy Fletcher?

Nun *Il signore Fletcher e morte.*

Luby What? Come?

Nun *Sta notte. E morte. Scusa, signore.*

Luby What?

Sophie Dead, Lewis. She told you he was dead.

He sits down hopelessly, looking at the empty bed

Luby Fletcher dead! And I'm alive. Harmlessly alive. You know what I have discovered? Everything *interesting* happens to Fletcher!

As Luby looks at Fletcher's bed the Lights fade on every area of the stage except for the empty bed, which remains lit until a quick Black-out, and—

the CURTAIN *falls*

FURNITURE AND PROPERTY LIST

On stage: 3 beds and bedding. *Beside* **Fletcher's:** oxygen cylinder
Set of screens to enclose two beds
3 bed tables. *On* **Young Italian's:** transistor radio. *On*
  Luby's: spectacles
Upright chair
Small table. *On it:* ashtray, knitting
  On ceiling: huge Italian painting of God and Heaven

Off stage: Glass bed-bottle **(Nun)**
Clipboard **(Nun)**

Personal: **Guide:** walking-stick, packet of cigarettes
Doctor: gold lighter

EFFECTS PLOT

Cue 1	**Young Italian** switches on radio *Music—"Madame Butterfly"*	(Page 4)
Cue 2	**Young Italian** switches off radio *Music off. Clock chimes the quarters*	(Page 4)
Cue 3	**Luby:** "It's a necessity." *Clock strikes One*	(Page 4)
Cue 4	**Luby:** ". . . let me back again." *Music—Gounods "Ave Maria"*	(Page 22)
Cue 5	**Young Italian** switches off radio *Music off*	(Page 22)

LIGHTING PLOT

Property fittings required: nil

Interior: A hospital ward

To open: Black-out

Cue 1	**After** CURTAIN **rises** *Bring up brilliant lighting on corner of ceiling*	(Page 1)
Cue 2	**Guide comes on stage** *Bring up gradual dim light on hospital beds*	(Page 1)
Cue 3	**Nun** and **Doctor remove screens** *Increase lighting over central beds*	(Page 2)
Cue 4	**After Guide exits** *Alter lighting quality to suggest passage of time*	(Page 4)
Cue 5	**Clock strikes** *Increase lighting on ceiling*	(Page 4)
Cue 6	**Luby pulls bedclothes over head** *Fade all lighting to very dim*	(Page 22)
Cue 7	**Nun draws screen round Fletcher's bed** *Fade to Black-out, then up to pale daylight: no lighting on ceiling*	(Page 22)
Cue 8	**Luby looks at Fletcher's bed** *Fade all lighting except spot on empty bed: follow with quick fade to Black-out*	(Page 26)